Two week loan

Please return on or before the last date stamped below.
Charges are made for late return.

Anti-Liberalism 2000

The Rise of New Millennium Collectivism

DAVID HENDERSON

THIRTIETH WINCOTT LECTURE 12 OCTOBER 2000

WITH COMMENTS BY G. C. HARCOURT

The Institute of Economic Affairs

335 H

First published in Great Britain in 2001 by
The Institute of Economic Affairs
2 Lord North Street
Westminster
London SW1P 3LB
in association with Profile Books Ltd

ISBN 0 255 36497 0

Many IEA publications are translated into languages other than English or are
reprinted. Permission to translate or to reprint should be sought from the
General Director at the address above.

Typeset in Stone by MacGuru
info@macguru.org.uk

Printed and bound in Great Britain by Hobbs the Printers

CONTENTS

THE AUTHORS

David Henderson was formerly (1984–92) Head of the Economics and Statistics Department of the Organisation for Economic Cooperation and Development (the OECD) in Paris. Before that he had worked as an academic economist in Britain, first in Oxford (Fellow of Lincoln College) and later in University College London (Professor of Economics), as a British civil servant (first as an Economic Adviser in HM Treasury, and later as Chief Economist in the UK Ministry of Aviation), and as a staff member of the World Bank. In 1985 he gave the BBC Reith Lectures, which were published in book form under the title of *Innocence and Design: The Influence of Economic Ideas on Policy* (Blackwell, 1986).

Since leaving the OECD he has been an independent author and consultant, and has acted as Visiting Fellow or Professor at the OECD Development Centre (Paris), the Centre for European Policy Studies (Brussels), Monash University (Melbourne), the Fondation Nationale des Sciences Politiques (Paris), the University of Melbourne, the Royal Institute of International Affairs (London), the New Zealand Business Roundtable, and the Melbourne Business School. Among his recent publications is *The Changing Fortunes of Economic Liberalism* (London, Institute of Economic Affairs, 1998, and Melbourne, 1999). He is an Honorary Fellow of Lincoln College, Oxford, and in 1992 he was made Commander of the Order of St Michael and St George.

Professor Emeritus G. C. Harcourt is a graduate of the Universities of Melbourne (B.Com Hons 1954, M.Com 1956) and Cambridge (Ph.D 1960, Litt.D 1988). He has taught at the Universities of Adelaide, Cambridge and Toronto. He is Emeritus Reader in the History of Economic Theory, Cambridge, Emeritus Fellow, Jesus College, Cambridge and Professor Emeritus, Adelaide University.

He has authored or co-authored, edited and co-edited 20 books and published over 170 papers in journals and books. His books include *Some Cambridge Controversies in the Theory of Capital* (1972), *A 'Second Edition' of The General Theory*, two volumes, edited with P. A. Riach, 1997, and seven volumes of selected essays. He was elected a Fellow of the Academy of the Social Sciences in Australia (FASSA) in 1971, made an Officer in the General Division of the Order of Australia (AO) in 1994 for 'Services to Economic Theory and the History of Economic Thought' and became '1996 Distinguished Fellow of the Economic Society of Australia' in 1996.

ACKNOWLEDGEMENTS

My thanks are due to the Wincott Trustees for honouring me with the invitation to give the 2000 Wincott Lecture. I would especially like to thank the Chairman of the Trustees, Sir Geoffrey Owen, for his helpful contributions at various stages of planning and preparation. The text that follows formed the basis for the lecture, but includes material which was left out of the talk itself. Drafting of the text was undertaken in two locations: first, the Groupe d'Economie Mondiale, directed by Professor Patrick Messerlin, in the Ecole Nationale des Sciences Politiques de Paris; and second, the Institute of Economic Affairs in London. I am grateful to the directors of both institutions for the facilities that they kindly provided, and to the IEA for publishing this text. Professor Len Shackleton, Dean of the Westminster Business School, made helpful comments on an earlier draft. Last, I would like to join the Wincott Trustees in thanking Dr Geoffrey Harcourt, who kindly agreed to open the discussion as an economist holding a different view from mine, for his contribution both to the occasion of the Lecture and to the present publication. I am very pleased that he was able and willing to accept the invitation to take on this role of critic-contributor.

DAVID HENDERSON
January 2001

FOREWORD

During the 1990s many commentators celebrated what they saw as the triumph of neo-liberal ideas in economic policy. A common view was that the old philosophy of collectivism and statism which had been so dominant in the early post-war decades was in headlong retreat. For a mixture of reasons, including the 'stagflation' of the 1970s and the example set in the following decade by Margaret Thatcher in Britain and Ronald Reagan in the US, policymakers throughout the world – in developing as well as developed countries – had recognised the advantages of free trade and the free movement of capital, and a reduced role for the government in the economy. A notable example was the emergence of 'New Labour' in Britain – an explicit rejection by the British Labour Party of the doctrines of nationalisation and state planning to which it had been committed in the past. Since coming into office in 1997, the Labour government led by Tony Blair has broadly accepted the Thatcherite legacy; far from reverting to the interventionism of the 1960s and 1970s, Labour ministers have been proclaiming the virtues of competition with all the enthusiasm of the convert.

All this would have delighted Harold Wincott, the great financial journalist in whose honour the Wincott Foundation was established in 1969. One of the central themes in his writings was the importance of allowing markets to work freely. His columns in the

Financial Times were influential and widely read, but, at a time when the collectivist tide was running strongly, he was a lonely voice. What happened in Britain after 1980 was in some ways a belated vindication of Harold Wincott's ideas.

Yet there are grounds for doubt. How solidly based is the conversion to liberalism? Socialism in the old sense may have lost its appeal, but that certainly does not mean that capitalism enjoys wholehearted and universal support. There are, indeed, powerful anti-capitalist forces at work. They are to be seen not only in the street protests which accompanied the World Trade Organization meeting in Seattle and the IMF meeting in Prague, but also in the activities of some non-governmental organisations (NGOs). Whether their concern is with environmental protection or the alleviation of poverty in developing countries, their rhetoric is tinged with more than a hint of anti-capitalist sentiment. These views are well represented in academia, and there is an increasing flow of books and articles dedicated to the proposition that 'globalisation' poses great dangers for the world.

There is, in short, a serious risk of an anti-liberal backlash, just as there was at the end of the nineteenth century. In these circumstances it is vitally important that the case for liberalism should be presented as clearly and forcefully as possible, and that the vacuity of many of the arguments levelled against it should be exposed. This is what Professor David Henderson aims to do in this paper – based on the Wincott Foundation lecture which he delivered at Church House, London, on 12 October 2000 – and he succeeds magnificently.

He points to the rise of what he calls new millennium collectivism, an amalgam of anti-liberal ideas promoted by a loose alliance which includes business groups, trade unions, NGOs, academics and most United Nations agencies. What gives the alliance its plausibility is its concern with obviously attractive objectives such as human rights, corporate social responsibility and sustainable development. But, as Henderson shows, the proposals which are put forward for meeting these objectives are based on economic arguments which are at best highly questionable and more often plain wrong.

This paper is in the best Wincottian tradition, a distinguished addition to the series of Wincott lectures which has been running annually since 1970. The trustees of the Wincott Foundation are grateful to David Henderson for agreeing to deliver the lecture, and to Geoff Harcourt for providing a most thoughtful and constructive response; this response, which provoked a lively debate in Church House, is published here along with the lecture. As in all IEA publications, the views expressed are those of the author, not of the Institute (which has no corporate view), its Managing Trustees, Academic Advisory Council members or senior staff.

SIR GEOFFREY OWEN

Chairman of the Trustees
The Wincott Foundation
November 2000

SUMMARY

- Over the last twenty to twenty-five years economic policies over most of the world have changed course: a growing number of governments have taken the path of liberalisation. Contrary to the view of some critics, this has made for better economic performance.
- The notion that economic liberalism has now triumphed is mistaken. Anti-liberal forces and influences remain strong, and on some fronts they have gained ground.
- Some aspects of anti-liberalism 2000 are not new. As always, interventionist policies are fuelled by the combined influence of interest groups and public opinion generally. A continuing factor here is the hold, even in informed circles, of pre-economic ideas. People think of a market economy as heavily populated by losers and victims, whose welfare depends on collective measures on the part of 'society'.
- These long-established anti-liberal influences have combined with more recent elements to form *new millennium collectivism*.
- Recent elements include the growing influence of anti-market NGOs (non-governmental organisations); a widening of the circle of those perceived as victims of injustice; the spread of labour market regulations which violate freedom of contract; and an alarmist consensus as to the impact of

globalisation and the state of the environment.

- These have given rise to proposals for new forms of interventionism, including closer international regulation of terms and conditions of employment which would be especially harmful to people in poor countries.
- New millennium collectivism covers a range of creeds and organisations, including radical groups that are strongly anti-liberal. Its main component is an informal but influential alliance embracing businesses, unions, the more moderate NGOs, academics, commentators and public figures, various elements in government circles, interventionist quangos and most UN agencies.
- The alliance derives much of its strength and appeal from three principles which though appealing are open to question as now interpreted. These are human rights, corporate social responsibility and sustainable development.
- Treasuries and ministries of finance, which are responsible for coordinating economic policies, have not responded effectively to the challenge of today's anti-liberalism.
- Some economist-critics have condemned the recent trend to more market-oriented economies as 'reactionary', but the reforms are not a return to the past. They were largely prompted by evidence of failure.
- It is not clear which of the reforms these critics would want to reverse, nor how far they would want to keep in place the many forms of interventionism that remain.
- The main impetus behind the anti-liberalism of today does not come from the writings of economists. It comes from the combination of interests, ideas and perceptions of the world that goes to make up new millennium collectivism.

Anti-Liberalism 2000

1 INTRODUCTION

Right through my professional life, I have been preoccupied
with economic policies and the factors that influence them. In particular, my interest lies in the changing balance within these policies between liberalism and interventionism. I have become a
chronicler of the changing fortunes of economic liberalism.

Here as elsewhere, I use the term 'liberalism' in its European
rather than its American sense. Hence a liberal is taken to be one
who emphasises the value of individual freedom, and who therefore judges measures and policies, economic as well as political,
primarily with reference to their effects on freedom. Economic liberalism favours policies that promote and enlarge economic freedom, both for their own sake and because they make for greater
prosperity.

In a recent study, I reviewed from this standpoint the economic history of the previous twenty years or so, from the end of
the 1970s to the late 1990s.[1] Here I look more closely at one of the
topics referred to there, namely, the various forces and influences

---

1 David Henderson, *The Changing Fortunes of Economic Liberalism: Yesterday, Today
and Tomorrow*, London, Institute of Economic Affairs, 1998 and Melbourne, Institute of Public Affairs and New Zealand Business Roundtable, 1999. At various
points below I have drawn on this book without specific acknowledgement, as
also from a forthcoming paper of mine which is to appear as a chapter in a book
of essays presented to Tony Killick, entitled *Development Economics in Africa and
the World*, to be published by Macmillan.

which now operate to prevent economic policies from becoming more liberal, or to make them less so. My subject is the anti-liberalism of today.

Under this heading, I try to cover

- Both new influences and older but still-continuing ones
- Both the world of action and that of ideas and doctrines
- As to ideas, not only the views and arguments of economists, but also a wider range. Economists typically overrate the extent to which economic policies are decided by what they think and write. Here I focus more on other influences.

In outlining the anti-liberal forces and influences of today, I say little about those that are pro-liberal. From a liberal standpoint, this makes for a sombre picture, which does not, however, pretend to be complete. Again, I do not try to assess how the balance of economic policies is likely to change, either immediately or in the longer term. I make no predictions, and present no scenarios. I consider anti-liberalism in itself and for its own sake.

Even with these omissions, what I can offer is no more than the barest sketch, though I have tried to avoid making the sketch into a caricature.

I realise that some of those I differ from might want to reject the unattractive-looking label of anti-liberal which I have pinned on them. Rather, they would see themselves as opposed to doctrinaire *laissez-faire* ideas and mistaken policies that are based on these. I use the label as convenient shorthand, no more.

I begin with some history, and then turn to the main anti-liberal forces and influences of today.

2 RECENT HISTORY: LIBERALISATION AND ITS SIGNIFICANCE

The recent history of economic policies is pertinent, not only as background, but also because it is a source of contention between liberals and anti-liberals.

Economic reform across the world

Over the past twenty to twenty-five years, the fortunes of economic liberalism have clearly improved. To an extent that was almost wholly unforeseen, a growing number of governments, at different stages, have taken steps to make national economies less regulated and flows of international trade and capital freer. In most countries, though by no means all, and in all the largest economies of the world, a process of market-oriented economic reform has been initiated and carried forward. The extent of reform has varied greatly, and as usual the make-up of economic policies has everywhere included both liberal and anti-liberal elements. But there is no doubting the general direction of change.

The trend is to be seen in all three of the main country groupings of twenty years ago – in all the OECD group, which then comprised 24 countries; in the developing countries including China; and, from the end of the 1980s, in countries of the former USSR and its satellites in central and eastern Europe.

For the OECD group in particular, dates are important. The story begins at the end of the 1970s – in the pre-Reagan US and the post-Thatcher UK. For most other OECD countries aside from Turkey, and for the group as a whole including the European Community, the shift in policies effectively dates from the early-to-mid 1980s. Everywhere, the process of reform extended over a number of years. In many countries it is still continuing.

Predictably, there is a long list of countries where governments have not liberalised. In some of these, the balance has actually shifted towards interventionism: Iran and Venezuela are leading examples. But the great majority of the non-reforming governments are from small economies in Africa, the Middle East and the former USSR. In Europe and on the American continent, and over much of Asia, non-reformers now appear as exceptional. Over the world as a whole, the reforming countries account for well over 90 per cent of total GDP.

Some of the current differences between liberals and anti-liberals relate to how these events should be viewed and interpreted. Let me comment on what I regard as some misinterpretations.

The myth of a 'conservative revolution'

A basic misconception is that this process of reform represents a 'conservative revolution'. Neither the noun nor the adjective is justified. 'Revolution' is too strong a term to describe what has typically involved no more than a shift in the balance of economic policies – albeit, in some cases, a profoundly significant shift. As to the label 'conservative', it is doubly out of place. In this recent period as in earlier phases of history, liberalisation has not necessarily, nor even predominantly, been associated with governments of the right. There have been many left-of-centre reforming governments, both in the OECD countries and elsewhere. In thus taking the path of reform, the political leaders concerned were not stealing their opponents' clothes. Liberalisation did not give expression to conservative ways of thinking, which in fact have never been well disposed towards economic liberalism.

Trends, timing and impact

A second mistaken view of the reforms is that they represent the continuation of a dominant long-run trend: political democracy and economic liberalism are seen – for example, by Francis Fukuyama in *The End of History and the Last Man* – as embodying the tide of history and the wave of the future. But over the 250 years or so that economic liberalism has existed as doctrine and programme, its fortunes have by no means been on a consistently rising trend. True, there was such a trend from the latter part of the eighteenth century onwards. But from the late nineteenth century the direction of change was reversed; and it remained, on balance, unfavourable to liberalism right up to, and in some countries well into, this latest phase. By the time that the recent improvement in its fortunes began to become general, in the early 1980s, *economic liberalism had been in decline for a hundred years*.

Nor is this all. Right at the end of this century-long evolution, from the early 1970s for a period which varied from case to case, the anti-liberal trend became stronger in many countries. This was especially true of the OECD group, where governments, chiefly in reaction to a worsening of the economic climate, resorted to a range of interventionist measures. These included:

- controls on prices and wages
- intergovernmental deals and state-directed programmes in energy markets
- bailing out (in some cases through nationalisation) of loss-making firms and industries
- increasing resort to illiberal forms of trade protection including in particular (so-called) voluntary export restraint agreements
- tighter foreign exchange controls
- closer restrictions on foreign direct investment.

I make this point because the history is sometimes oversimplified by critics of reform. As a result, liberalisation is blamed for developments in which it played no part, and which indeed it might have helped to mitigate or prevent.

In all the OECD countries, economic performance deteriorated in the early 1970s. But this cannot be attributed to liberalisation, which in every case came years later. Take for example the rise in unemployment rates. Geoffrey Harcourt, in a 1998 article, includes in a list of 'the happenings of the past 20–25 years or so' 'the emergence of sustained mass unemployment in many advanced countries'.[1] But unemployment rates had risen markedly in most OECD countries well before the process of reform set in: Geoff's native Australia is one of the clearest examples. Here economic policies changed course, so that the balance shifted decisively away from interventionism, only right at the end of 1983. For the year 1983, just before this break occurred, the Australian unemployment rate was

---

1 Geoffrey Harcourt, 'Political Economy, Politics and Religion: Intertwined and Indissoluble Passions', *The American Economist*, Vol. 42, No. 2, Fall 1998.

already just under 10 per cent, as compared with only 2.3 per cent ten years earlier. For 1999, following a fifteen-year period which broadly had been one of liberalisation, it stood at 7.2 per cent.

It is true that in a number of OECD countries, almost all in continental Europe, the high unemployment rates which preceded liberalisation have persisted through to the present day. But recent work by the OECD Secretariat indicates that it is the failure by governments to make labour markets freer that is largely responsible for this persistence.[2]

Another misplaced argument against liberalisation relates to the general stability of economies in which it has gone ahead. Here again, let me quote Geoff Harcourt. In an earlier article, he blamed 'the deregulation of financial markets and the consequent huge expansion of credit facilities for all' for what he saw as 'The greatly increased amplitude of fluctuations in spending, and the increased length of slumps'.[3] But in the OECD economies at any rate, there is little sign of such developments in the period that is relevant – that is, the last fifteen years or so. For the group as a whole over this period, there has been no slump, nor even a recession that shows up in annual data. GDP has risen by some 50 per cent, and further increases are in prospect for this year and next. At the same time, the average inflation rate for the group has come down, and the area-wide unemployment rate was slightly lower in 1999 than in 1984. Right through the period, the year-on-year change in GDP was positive for the group as a whole, whereas there had been two years in the previous decade for which this was not the case. These

---

2   Evidence on this is to be found in the work carried out over the past seven years or so within the OECD Jobs Study.

3   Geoffrey Harcourt, 'Markets, Madness and a Middle Way', Donald Horne Address 1992, published in *Australian Quarterly*, Vol. 64, Autumn 1992.

results compare favourably with those of the decade from the early 1970s to the early 1980s.

To repeat: the worsening of the economic situation in OECD countries in the early 1970s cannot be attributed to liberalisation. I would argue that, on the contrary, it can more justly be seen as due in part if not largely to anti-liberal policies. These were put in place both before and after the worsening began.[4]

The myth of a 'neo-liberal hegemony'

Many critics of the reform process believe that doctrinaire liberalism has been taken to extremes and that it now reigns supreme: some of them refer gloomily to what they call 'a neo-liberal hegemony'. On the other side of the ideological fence, I just read a paper by a member of the British Conservative Party's present Shadow Cabinet which claims that 'The free market has emerged triumphant, accepted once again everywhere as the natural condition of mankind'.[5] Both the gloom and the celebrations are overdone: economic liberalism is far from having won the day. This is chiefly because of the continuing power and influence of anti-liberalism, which is my main theme today. Before turning to it, however, let me make two points just on the recent history.

Point One

In every country, including the most radical reformers, there are

---

4   This is the main theme of an OECD Secretariat report of 1987, which still repays reading, entitled *Structural Adjustment and Economic Performance*.

5   Oliver Letwin, 'Civilised Conservatism', in *Conservative Debates*, London, Politeia, 1999, p. 1.

large areas of economic policy where interventionist assumptions and practice have been little affected, and some fronts on which liberalism has arguably lost ground.

- Generally speaking, liberalisation has not been extended to those goods and services which remain largely outside the market economy. Almost everywhere, education, health and the delivery of social services are still dominated by state provision as well as state financing
- Even in the sphere of marketed output, highly illiberal forms of intervention can still be found. Examples are (1) the agricultural policies of most OECD countries (other than Australia and New Zealand), and (2) the many restrictions that remain in place on international trade and direct investment flows
- Alongside privatisation and deregulation in particular industries and sectors, more restrictive economy-wide regulations have been imposed in many countries. The areas chiefly affected are the environment, occupational health and safety, and terms and conditions of hiring and employment.

Point Two

Few if any reforming governments were consciously and consistently liberal. This was true even of the governments presided over in Britain by Mrs Thatcher in the years 1979–90, despite all that was done in that period by way of 'rolling back the frontiers of the state'. Until well into the 1980s, policies in relation to energy, industry and – especially – international trade largely conformed to the interventionist patterns set by past British governments of differing political complexions. As time went on, and thinking and policy evolved further, liberalisation went ahead in both energy and industry policies; but science policy stayed firmly *dirigiste* throughout these years and afterwards. As to trade policies, as late as 1987 two well-informed commentators could write that:

> It is not difficult to find out who the protectionist and non-protectionist members of the [European] Community are: the EC Council alignment in debates on trade policy for manufactures never varies. The Netherlands, the Federal Republic of Germany and Denmark are for free trade, the UK, France and Italy for a restrictive policy.[6]

Admittedly, this too was to change as still more time went by. On the other hand – and here there was no change – Mrs Thatcher's governments, and she herself, consistently lent their support, and in some cases provided critical financial backing, in specific export deals where British firms were involved: the affair of the Pergau Dam is a well-known instance. Along with other governments all over the world, and regardless of political colouring, British governments in this respect have to this day remained staunchly mercantilist.

The fact is that economic liberals always were, and still are, thin on the ground. There is no 'neo-liberal hegemony', nor has the idea of a free economy 'emerged triumphant'. In few if any countries today is there a political party of any significance which is identified with the cause of economic liberalism. Now as ever, liberalism, both as doctrine and as a programme of action, occupies ground that is strongly contested. I now turn to review some of its opponents in the contest.

6   Jean Waelbroeck and Jacob Koz, 'Export Opportunities for the South in the Evolving Pattern of World Trade', Centre for Economic Policy Studies (Brussels), Report No. 33, 1987.

3 ANTI-LIBERALISM: OLD INFLUENCES IN TODAY'S SETTING

The coming together of interests and perceptions

Two related anti-liberal influences are long established but still going strong. One comprises the activities of interest groups. In the great majority of cases, such groups are anti-liberal in effect, even though they may have no interest in economic doctrines. Some of them, like the agriculturalists in OECD countries, are arguing against forms of liberalisation which would make them worse off. Others, like the American and European firms that lobby for anti-dumping duties, or the recent European campaigners against higher fuel prices, want special government concessions, assistance or protection from competition. They are pragmatic interventionists.

The tendency in both economics and political science today is to emphasise the power of such groups. They are seen as colluding, in a dominant unholy triple alliance, with political leaders and government officials who are likewise taken to be self-interested, rationally calculating and opportunist. Hence there is said to be a built-in trend to interventionism. Ordinary citizens and voters, even though they stand to lose if the interest groups get their way, are seen as having too little at stake, in each individual case, to incur the costs of informing themselves on the issues and mobilising countervailing pressures. They remain non-participants, in a state of 'rational ignorance'.

I believe that this line of argument, though it throws light on some aspects of history, is overdone and incomplete. Its portrayal of political and official life is at best an approximation and at worst a caricature. It also fails to account for actual events. On the back cover of my *Changing Fortunes of Economic Liberalism* there is a ten-point summary of the argument. Point 6 reads:

> It is not true that coalitions of interests largely preclude economic liberalisation: otherwise, the reforms of recent years would not have taken place.

The same is true in relation to earlier episodes of reform: I find it hard to think of any leading historical instance of liberalisation which can be accounted for in terms of the combined influence of interest groups and their rationally compliant allies in the corridors of power.

Admittedly, when it comes to interventionist moves and trends, or successful opposition to reforms, this combined influence has often been considerable or even decisive. But in these cases also, the search for explanations may have to be extended more widely.

In my view, it is often necessary to take account of the views and perceptions of those outside the so-called 'iron triangle', views and perceptions which may well be shared by politicians and officials within it. Interest groups are successful not just through skilful lobbying and persuasion directed towards those in power, but also by winning assent or support from a wider public opinion, made up of those who are outside the process of decision-making and whose jobs and incomes are not at stake in what is decided. People are not necessarily indifferent about issues which do not closely and directly involve them, and which they have neither time nor inclination to inquire into. Typical voters, and even typical ministers and officials, have ideas and opinions concerning what is fair, just and acceptable, and as to what actions are likely to promote social or national goals of which they approve. When this is so, the views of outsiders can carry weight.

I recently found support for this view of mine in the work of the Chicago legal scholar, Richard Epstein. Writing about the growth of regulation, Epstein argues as follows:

> Why the constant push to legal complexity ...? In part the explanation lies in the inexorable pressures exerted by innumerable special interest groups. But in addition, *ideas are at work that lead the vast mass of disinterested people to keep a receptive ear open to the claims of regulation* ... [One such idea] is the innocent but often fatal impulse to achieve perfect justice in the individual case. [A] second is the false belief that the complex forms of regulation which work within small voluntary groups can be duplicated in large, impersonal social settings.[1]

The same is true for economic policies: ideas are at work which make disinterested people receptive to interventionism. In fact, I would argue that *characteristic majority attitudes towards economic issues are anti-liberal.* Hence there is often a coming together of interests and outside perceptions. Now as in the past, policies are often steered in an interventionist direction by the combined influence of anti-liberal interest groups and anti-liberal outside opinion.

---

1   Richard Epstein, *Simple Rules for a Complex World*, Cambridge, MA, Harvard University Press, 1992, p. 37; italics added.

The influence of do-it-yourself economics

What makes outside opinion anti-liberal? In the book that I just quoted from, Richard Epstein takes the view that it is oversimplified ideas concerning justice and the law that lead disinterested persons to favour regulation. In many issues of economic policy, an analogous influence is to be found in questionable but firmly held ideas about economic events, relationships and goals. These notions are largely intuitive, and can justly be termed 'pre-economic'. I have labelled this way of thinking 'do-it-yourself economics' (DIYE), and I made it the theme of my 1985 BBC Reith Lectures.[2] Here I would like to note two points relating to it.

First, what is in question here is not just 'popular economic fallacies', the uninstructed beliefs of ordinary and unimportant people. These same notions are held with equal conviction, and expressed in much the same language, by political leaders, top civil servants, chief executives of businesses, general secretaries of trade unions, well-known journalists and commentators, religious leaders, senior judges and eminent professors – as also, on occasion, by economists themselves. Recent additions to my long list of DIYE exponents in Britain include an earl, a knight, a pro-free trade professor of economics, the Archbishop of Canterbury and the late Poet Laureate. Beyond these shores, I have just included the current President of the World Bank.

Second, DIYE is staunchly interventionist. Consider for example a few of its characteristic doctrines:

---

2   David Henderson, *Innocence and Design: The influence of economic ideas on policy*, Oxford, Blackwell, 1986.

- that industries or activities can be classed as either 'essential' or 'non-essential', or ranked in order of priority
- that governments should ensure self-sufficiency in essentials, and provide systematic support to products, industries and sectors which have high priority
- that when transactions take place across national boundaries, the state is involved, so that international competition is primarily between states
- that exports represent a gain to each country, and imports a loss
- that tariffs, import restrictions and export subsidies serve to increase total employment
- that administrative actions to reduce or constrain the size of the labour force – such as compulsory reductions in working hours, enforced early retirement, or tighter restrictions on immigration – will ease the problem of unemployment
- that actions undertaken for profit, or more broadly from self-interest, are open to question as such.

All these propositions, and others I could list which likewise point towards interventionism, are widely held. They carry weight despite the fact that, so far as one can generalise about our chronically disordered profession, most economists would not be comfortable with them. The discomfort arises from what I call a professional *semi-consensus* on the functioning and uses of markets and prices. Anti-liberals as well as liberals may subscribe to this semi-consensus.

Hence I was not surprised to see Geoff Harcourt writing, in his 1992 article already quoted, of 'the advantages and achievements' of 'markets and competitive forces'. To this extent though no further, he is to be counted, if he will pardon the expression, as One of Us.[3]

The economic reforms of recent years have in fact given expression to ideas which are characteristic of economists as of no other group. Although many economists even today, quite possibly a majority, would not wish to describe themselves as liberals in my sense of the term, the fact is that liberals are more likely to be found within their ranks than outside them. Conversely, anti-liberal views today are often associated, as in the days of Coleridge and Carlyle and Ruskin, with hostility to economics and some of its characteristic ways of thinking.

This, however, is not the whole picture. There are some other widely held intuitive economic ideas where the professionals are more divided. Many of them would be prepared to endorse, perhaps with some redrafting, these three DIYE propositions:

- that extending the scope of markets is liable to increase the extent of unpredictability and instability within economic systems, and of insecurity for the people who live and work in them
- that within countries, 'unfettered' market processes favour the rich and powerful, rather than the poor, so that typically their outcomes are arbitrary and unjust
- that freedom of international trade and direct investment flows places poor countries at a disadvantage, relatively if not absolutely.

---

3   On consensus among economists and its limits, an illuminating treatment is to be found in Samuel Brittan, *Is There an Economic Consensus? An attitude survey*, London, Macmillan, 1973.

Non-beneficiaries, victims and deliverance from above

Acceptance of these propositions often goes with an anti-liberal view of economic history. According to this, the achievement over time of higher material welfare for ordinary people is to be attributed not so much to increases in productivity and output per head, but rather to the impact of trade unions, the closer regulation of wages and conditions of employment, and the development of social legislation and progressive taxation systems. An extreme variant of this is the belief that the *only* way in which ordinary people can become better off is through government-directed programmes to raise their status or transfer resources to them: the record of past and current economic growth is simply disregarded. A less extreme variant holds that in an 'unfettered' market economy the fruits of economic growth typically accrue to the rich and powerful. Hence others will benefit from growth only in so far as there is a process of 'trickle-down' from richer to poorer, which is not to be relied on.

In this sombre picture of the world, a market economy, even a well-performing one, is heavily populated with *non-beneficiaries and victims*. For whole classes of people, for whole nations and countries, prospects for a better life are seen as contingent above all on collective action, either to influence market outcomes or to redress their effects. Their well-being depends on *deliverance from above*. Within national boundaries, the responsibility for providing this is seen as falling to 'society'.[4] For the world as a whole, it is

---

4 This theme has been developed in a number of the writings of Thomas Sowell. For example, he has noted (in *Ethnic America: A History*, New York, Basic Books, 1981, p. 296), in relation to different ethnic groups, that 'Within the confines of the moralistic approach, progress (like poverty) can only be presented as a product of "society" – now grudgingly granting new "rights" or partial "acceptance"'.

now increasingly attributed to 'the international community'.

This vision, though not new, has recently acquired some new aspects. The two combine to make up what I call *new millennium collectivism*.

4   NEW MILLENNIUM COLLECTIVISM

Developments in both the realm of action and the realm of ideas have come together to give the anti-liberalism of today its special character.

The rise of the NGOs

First and foremost among these developments is the rise of the NGOs. These are non-governmental organisations – hence the initials – but they are distinct from other organisations which are likewise non-governmental, such as groups representing businesses, professions or trade unions. They stand not for particular sectional interests, but for causes. Hence they are often given the tactically useful label of 'public interest' groups. They include consumer associations, conservation and environmental groups, societies concerned with development in poor countries, human rights groups, movements for social justice, humanitarian societies, organisations representing indigenous peoples, and church groups from all denominations. They are now often classed together, misleadingly, under the heading of 'civil society'. This label also is tactically useful.

Although the NGOs are largely based in the OECD countries, they have now become an influential element on the world scene. Almost everywhere, they have been brought by governments and international agencies into more or less formal consultative processes. Many have been assigned roles as executing agencies for official aid projects. For this and other reasons, many receive official financing. Businesses generally, and large multinational enterprises in particular, go out of their way to inform, consult and where possible cooperate with them. In the recent case of the proposed – and ill-fated – Multilateral Agreement on Investment (MAI), NGOs from many countries came together, using the internet as a means of communication and coordination, to conduct a well-orchestrated campaign against the proposal.[1] They now have a recognised place in many international meetings, and there are proposals for expanding their role. In the fruitless Seattle meeting of the World Trade Organization at the end of last year, many representatives of NGOs were officially present as invited observers, and in some cases actually as delegates. Other groups, more extreme in their views, ran street demonstrations against the whole proceedings, as they have more recently in Prague.

Generally speaking, the NGOs are anti-liberal. With some exceptions, they are hostile to, or highly critical of, capitalism, multinational enterprises, freedom of cross-border trade and capital flows, and the idea of a market economy. They are a force on the side of interventionism.

Widening the circle of victims

In the realm of ideas, as distinct from the realm of action, anti-liberalism 2000 differs from its counterpart of twenty to twenty-five years ago in three main respects.

---

1   It is not correct, however, that the NGOs were responsible for the failure to conclude the MAI. OECD governments brought the negotiations to an end for their own reasons.

- First, its various adherents now include few, if any, who believe in the superiority of systems based on Soviet-style or Maoist state-directed economic planning: that issue at any rate appears to have been settled.
- Second, there is naturally a range of anti-liberal criticisms of the economic reform process that has been under way: I referred above to one or two of these, but there are other aspects that I have left untouched. More of this later.
- Last, and the most influential of the three, the circle of supposed non-beneficiaries and victims has been widened; and within it, some of the non-beneficiaries have been reclassified as victims. As a result, the grounds for intervention have been further extended. Let me illustrate this point, and show how long-established forms of anti-liberal thinking and practice have been taking on new features.

Labour market policies

A central area of policy, in which both older and newer anti-liberal elements are to be seen, is that of labour markets. Some recent developments, such as the 35-hour week introduced in France, fall into a long-established pattern. Alongside these, however, is a further category of regulations which belongs to the modern era: the main initial steps were taken in the 1970s, but there have been later additions. I refer here to laws concerning equal opportunity, anti-discrimination, human rights and affirmative action in the workplace. These are based on the notion that perceived inequalities in employment outcomes are evidence of wrongful discrimination. This presumption has defined whole new categories of possible victims.

Present-day labour laws typically embody both forms of regulation, traditional and modern. Here is a recent summary of the situation that has now been established in South Africa.

> Minimum wages are negotiated between unions and the larger firms in an industry, and then extended to smaller firms in the same industry, whether they were party to the agreement or not …. this creates a lofty barrier to entry for small start-up businesses. Minimum wages are typically set at about twice what the army of unemployed would accept.
>
> On top of this, employers must grant maternity leave, increase overtime rates, raise the proportion of blacks, women and disabled people in managerial jobs, and pay a 'skills levy' which can be reimbursed only if the firm spends money on government-approved training schemes …. When sacking staff or retrenching, bosses must follow long and complex procedures to the letter. A small technical violation of these procedures can lead to awards of up to a year's salary to each employee involved. It is easy for employees to bring complaints before arbitrators, so South Africa's arbitrators have a long and growing backlog.
> (*The Economist*, 29 July 2000)

One effect of all this is to raise the costs of doing business, from which everyone in the community, rich or poor, is liable to be made worse off. But a further and more fundamental concern is that such a regime is anti-liberal, because of the ways in which it violates the principle of freedom of contract – the principle that people should be free to enter into non-coercive bargains and arrangements for mutual gain. Laws and regulations of the kind just described restrict this freedom: they narrow the range of choices and opportunities available to workers and employers alike. Those whose interests are damaged by such denials of opportunity typically include, as in the South African case, the worst-off members of the labour force. Nearer home, there is the instance of Germany following reunification, where employment opportunities in the former communist *Länder* have been destroyed on a grand scale by the phased elimination of wage differences between east and west.

The supposed impact of globalisation

One recent but now characteristic element in anti-liberalism 2000 is a starkly melodramatic view of globalisation and its effects. Globalisation is often portrayed, quite misleadingly, as a newly arisen economic tidal wave which is sweeping peoples and governments before it and creating an anarchic borderless world. In this supposed new world, national governments are losing control, while newly empowered multinational enterprises are increasingly able to decide outcomes, and to exploit workers and keep down environmental standards, in a growing range of countries. For many people, these developments are seen as intensifying already serious threats to the environment, threats chiefly arising from market-driven transactions: the earth itself, and various ecosystems within it, are classed among the victims of the present economic system.

Beliefs of this kind are held by many if not most NGOs; by numerous academics; by journalists, commentators, parliamentarians, and public figures who express opinions on these matters; by a range of international agencies; and also, increasingly, by business leaders, business organisations, and writers on business affairs. Across the world, though more in the OECD countries than elsewhere, there has developed a wide-ranging and highly influential *alarmist consensus*, which stresses the need for collective action.

Globalisation is seen as having swelled the ranks of losers and victims everywhere, especially though by no means only in poor countries. This has been a principal recent theme of the *Human Development Report*, the influential annual series brought out by the United Nations Development Programme (UNDP). Last year's Report in particular dwelt on what it referred to as 'the negative effects of globalization – growing marginalization of poor countries and poor people, growing insecurity and growing inequality'.[2]

The main evidence of 'marginalisation' is that in a long list of mostly poor countries, levels of GDP per head, and of material welfare generally, have fallen further behind those of the rich countries of the world: in this respect, disparities that were already large have increased. The widening gap between the better off and the worse off is treated as a critical, a dominant problem. The same preoccupation with disparities is also to be seen in other contexts – for example, the distribution of income or earnings within countries, comparative indicators of health and mortality, and the perceived inequalities that I mentioned already, which have given rise to equal opportunity and anti-discrimination laws.

---

2 United Nations Development Programme, *Human Development Report 1999*, New York, United Nations, 1999. The passage quoted is from the opening sentence of the official press release. I reviewed the Report in 'False Perspective: The UNDP View of the World', published in *World Economics*, January–March 2000. A reply to this article by Richard Jolly appears in the issue of *World Economics* for July–September 2000, under the title, 'False Attack'.

The presumption of injustice

In all this, there is a common presumption. It is *that the existence of large disparities is an evil, and that it gives proof of remediable injustice*. It is this belief, in conjunction with the alarmist consensus, that provides the main doctrinal basis for anti-liberalism 2000.

The presumption of injustice is reflected in a now standard vocabulary. Take the *Human Development Report 1999*. Although 'marginalised' is its favourite term, reference is also made to countries being 'deprived', 'excluded', 'condemned' and 'disenfranchised' [*sic*], and to their status as 'victims'. That disparities have widened is seen as reason in itself to attribute blame to the international economic system and to recent changes within it: these are seen as having inflicted actual harm.

The same note of condemnation is struck in other contexts. In Britain, 'deprivation' and 'social exclusion' are now formally recognised as central problems that governments must address. When a recent report found that average income per head in Cornwall was well below that for Southern England generally, the minister concerned, Mr Prescott, at once drew the conclusion that Cornish people are deprived. I doubt whether his shadow spokesperson on the Opposition front bench would have seen anything odd in this use of language. Often, the remedy for deprivation and social exclusion is now seen to lie in 'empowering' those involved: empowerment is today's formula for deliverance from above.

So strong is the presumption of injustice that arguments and evidence to the contrary are often set aside. Consider for example the poor countries that have fallen further behind in recent years. Probably not one of them would now be better off, and some might be worse off, if growth elsewhere in the world had been slower, in which case the gap would have widened less. What really matters is not the gap as such, but the progress of these countries. As to why their recent progress has been so limited, it is clear that in the great majority of cases, perhaps all of them, internal factors have been important if not decisive. Many of the countries have been subject, in different ways, to conflict, disorder and chronic misgovernment. In most of these, and in some other countries too, growth has been held back by the economic policies that governments have chosen to pursue, including in particular policies which have kept their economies relatively closed to the outside world. It is wrong to present globalisation as a reason why growth has not gone ahead faster in such varied cases such as Cuba, North Korea, Afghanistan, Iran, Nigeria, Sierra Leone, Zimbabwe, Haiti or Papua New Guinea. All these obvious facts are played down or disregarded by many commentators, because of the wish to portray non-beneficiaries as victims of the system. Again, the fact that over the past twenty to twenty-five years economic performance has been notably good in China, largely because of market-oriented economic reforms, is likewise played down because it conflicts with the idea that deliverance has to come from above. A similar treatment of evidence can be found in other areas of presumed 'marginalisation' and injustice.

Regulating the world

Widening the circle of victims and assigning blame to the operation of 'unfettered' markets point the way to a range of interventionist measures and programmes. I have already touched on labour laws and regulations within countries. But there are also proposals for regulating the world as a whole.

Among these, I shall mention now only measures relating to terms and conditions of employment. What is chiefly involved here is action, whether official or unofficial, to establish and enforce minimum international labour standards. This is often linked to the aim of defining and giving effect to an ever-growing list of so-called 'positive' human rights.

Recent official action on these lines is to be seen in the Social Chapter of the European Union and in one of the side agreements of the North American Free Trade Agreement. Both the US and the European Union are now pressing for clauses relating to labour standards to be included in future international agreements relating to trade and direct investment. Such proposals have been attacked, I think with good reason, by liberal economists. However – and I think this is not as yet widely recognised – the risks here do not arise from official measures alone. Even without intergovernmental agreements, similar effects can result from decisions taken on their own account by multinational enterprises. These firms are now under strong pressure from public opinion generally, and NGOs in particular, to ensure that terms and conditions of employment, not only in their own operations but also in those of their partners and suppliers, are acceptable. A large and growing number of multinationals have now made explicit commitments of this kind, as also in relation to environmental standards where there are similar pressures; and they are acting in this way not just in response to pressure but also in the belief that they are doing the right thing. Increasingly, they publish information about their performance under these headings, and subject themselves to various forms of audit and inspection.

By way of illustration, here is a leading business advocate of 'corporate social responsibility' as that term is now interpreted. A recently-published volume in the *Financial Times* series on management, entitled *Corporate Citizenship: successful strategies for responsible companies*, has an approving foreword by Alice Tepper Marlin, President of the Council on Economic Priorities in the US. Here she sounds a note of alarm. She writes that 'as assembly and manufacturing jobs move in response to market conditions, children and impoverished adults are hired at rock-bottom wages'.[3] It seems not to have occurred to her, nor to those who think like her, that the adults who voluntarily seek employment with foreign-connected firms, on terms that they are aware of, do so in the hope and expectation of becoming less impoverished. Likewise, it seems not to have occurred to her and those like her that, at the wage levels they are prepared to approve for others, job opportunities may be closed off. Just as unemployed east Germans may be denied the freedom to work except on the terms that prevail in the west, and unemployed South Africans to take jobs that they would like to have at rates below those in industry agreements, so people in poor countries generally, for their own good of course, and in the name of human rights and minimum labour standards, must be denied the possibility of entering into deals with foreign firms which they believe would make them better off, but which would involve wages that would be condemned as 'rock-bottom' by European, American and Australasian television viewers, trade unionists, NGOs, commentators and public figures, and advocates of corporate social responsibility. In such cases, with or without official regulations, freedom of contract is suppressed.

This example shows that to defend and enlarge economic free-

---

3   Malcolm McIntosh and others, *Corporate Citizenship: Successful strategies for responsible companies*, London, *Financial Times* and Pitman Publishing, 1998.

dom involves more than limiting the role of government: businesses, in conjunction with NGOs, can carve out a role of their own
in regulating the world, and many of them are now ready to do this.
But even then, governments are liable to become involved. Large
multinationals could well find that that they are incurring higher
costs through assuming the responsibilities of corporate citizenship, while some of their unregenerate competitors are escaping
this burden. They then have a strong incentive to see to it that the
nonconformists are brought into line, and made into good corporate citizens, if not by public opinion then by official measures,
through domestic legislation or international agreements. The
possible need for regulation was underlined not long ago by Sir
John Browne, Chief Executive Officer of BP Amoco. He argued that

> Only national governments, individually and collectively,
> can set the standards which ensure that those who behave in
> ethical and transparent ways are not undercut by those who
> don't.[4]

Militants and mainstream

Within the ranks of new millennium collectivists, there are dis-
parate and sometimes warring elements. Broadly, one can distin-
guish between a radical wing, the zealots or militants, and those to
be found in the main body. On my own rough and ready classifi-
cation, the militants come under four main headings:

- 'dark green' environmentalists, who wish to assert the rights

---

4   Sir John Browne, 'International Relations: the new agenda for business', Elliott
    Lecture, St Anthony's College, Oxford, 1998.

of other living creatures, and the earth as a whole, against
what they view as the damaging and destructive activities of
human beings

- radical egalitarians, whose concern is to put an end to a whole
range of differences and disparities perceived as unjust
- all-out anti-globalists, who advocate a return to what appears
to be a modern version of the medieval manorial economy
- many if not most disciples of post-modernism, who reject
what they see as the culture of transnational capitalism.

Despite differences of interest and emphasis, these groups
broadly share a vision of the world in which past history and present-day market-based economic systems are portrayed in terms
of patterns of oppression and abuses of power. Free markets and
capitalism are seen as embodying and furthering environmental
destruction, male dominance, class oppression, racial intolerance,
imperialist coercion and colonialist exploitation. The prevalence
and the appeal of these deeply anti-liberal attitudes has been little
affected by the collapse of communism, which might just as well
have taken place on another planet.

Although such groups and their ways of thinking are not now
well represented in the corridors of power, they are not at all to be
dismissed as insignificant. Among their members all have votes,
many are vocal and active, and some are well represented, in lobbying and public debate, through NGOs.

Alongside the radicals, and on some issues in sympathy with
them, is the informal but wide-ranging and influential alliance
which now makes up mainstream anti-liberal thought and action.
It comprises businesses and business organisations, unions, the
more moderate NGOs, commentators and public figures includ-

ing parliamentarians, political leaders and civil servants in a good many government departments, a range of interventionist quangos, and most UN agencies.

Illiberal virtue

One reason for the strength of the alliance, and its breadth of membership, is that its doctrines incorporate three highly appealing interrelated concepts: human rights, corporate social responsibility and sustainable development. All three appear, and are presented, as proof against doubts or objections: who could want to oppose, deny or restrict human rights, to prefer that corporations should act non-responsibly, or to advocate development that was unsustainable? Yet all these virtuous-seeming notions, as now interpreted, bear a collectivist message.

From a liberal viewpoint, extending the list of 'positive' social and economic rights, whether through legislation or by adding to the long succession of UN declarations and resolutions on the subject, is not a sign of progress. At best it has no point, since (to quote Hayek) 'It is meaningless to speak of a right to a condition which nobody has the duty, or perhaps even the power, to bring about'.[5] At worst, it may do actual harm, by misdirecting attention and by lending impetus to proposals for regulating the world in the name of higher standards.

The currently accepted doctrine of corporate social responsibility (CSR), as now interpreted by many multinational enterprises and by outside writers and commentators, is worrying from

---

5   In *Law, Legislation and Liberty*, Vol. 2, *The Mirage of Social Justice*, London, Routledge and Kegan Paul, 1976, p. 102.

a liberal point of view despite the fact that it has its main origin in challenges that companies had to respond to. Most of those who subscribe to it – businesses, business organisations, business-supported foundations and think-tanks, academics in business schools and a growing array of eager consultants and advisers – are keen new millennium collectivists. They are part of the alarmist consensus on threats to the environment and the dire effects of globalisation; and with few exceptions, they accept a dual-aspect anti-liberal thesis.

- Aspect One is that business should now join with governments, 'civil society' and international agencies in rescuing a world beset with problems, dangers and sources of injustice, where the power to decide and act is passing from governments to corporations.
- Aspect Two is that this implies a radical rethinking of the role and functioning of business and the working of a market economy: capitalism has to be made anew.

I am now in the course of finishing an essay on this subject, entitled 'Misguided virtue: false notions of corporate social responsibility'. Working through the background reading for this, the writings of those in and around the business world who favour CSR, has proved a truly depressing task. Had the title not been already used by Robert Halfon, I might have been tempted to call my essay 'Corporate Irresponsibility'.[6]

The advocates of CSR are apt to present it as giving effect to the universally accepted and unchallengeable principle of sustainable

6   Robert Halfon, 'Corporate Irresponsibility: Is business appeasing anti-business activists?', London, Social Affairs Unit, 1998.

development. It is indeed true that this principle is now widely accepted, by governments as well as in unofficial circles: a recent instance is last year's OECD Ministerial Communique, which includes the statement that 'The pursuit of sustainable development … . is a key objective for OECD countries'. But the term is neither well defined nor above criticism. Among other things, the assertion is repeatedly made that sustainable development has three aspects or dimensions – economic, environmental and social. But the nature and rationale of this threefold division are unclear; and when it comes to the point, the environmental aspect is often identified with the alarmist consensus and the social aspect with 'social justice' defined in terms of perceived disparities and long lists of designated victims. Like human rights and corporate social responsibility, sustainable development has become a way of dressing up new millennium collectivism.

Failure at the centre?

In the work that I have done on different aspects of anti-liberalism over the past few years, I have been struck by the apparent weakness of the resistance to it within OECD governments. I think there has been a failure here on the part of the central departments or agencies – normally treasuries, ministries of finance, or ministries of economics – that carry the responsibility for providing leadership and direction to economic policies as a whole. I have the impression, based on reasonably close and continuous observation, albeit now as an outsider, that in face of the new manifestations of anti-liberalism these central economic departments have been inactive and unresourceful, even to the point of acquiescence. This may be partly explained by a failure to grasp what is happening.

5 RIVAL VISIONS

Last, a word on the arguments among economists and their significance today.[1]

Middle Way or Third Way?

To start with, there is a question of labelling. Geoffrey Harcourt has described his own position as constituting a 'middle way' between 'command and market, free-for-all, economies'. However, I note that he is an open admirer of Adam Smith, as is another anti-liberal economist whom I admire, Paul Streeten. I would argue that any appreciative reader of Smith is either a paid-up or an honorary member of the economists' semi-consensus, and hence a good deal closer to Margaret Thatcher than to Chairman Mao. I would therefore suggest to Geoff that, provided he has no problem with the company he would then be keeping, he should define his position in terms, not of a 'middle way', but of a 'third way'.

Progress and reaction

In a lecture series some years ago, Paul Streeten ended with a sec-

---

1   After drafting this final section, I read Thomas Sowell's book, *A Conflict of Visions* (New York, Basic Books, 1987), and realised that I was in effect developing a further variation on its theme.

tion headed 'The struggle for human progress'. There he deployed an argument taken from Albert Hirschman's book, *The Rhetoric of Reaction*.[2] Hirschman himself gives as his source Rolf Dahrendorf, who in his turn had given the credit to a former Professor of Sociology at LSE, T. H. Marshall. As set out by Streeten, the main argument runs as follows.

> It has taken the more enlightened advanced societies three centuries to achieve the civil, political and social dimensions of human development. The eighteenth century established *civil* rights . . . . In the course of the nineteenth century *political* freedom and participation in the exercise of political power made major strides as the right to vote was extended to more people. In the twentieth century the welfare state extended human development to the *social* and *economic* sphere, by recognizing that minimum standards of education, health, nutrition, well-being and security are basic to the civilized life, as well as to the exercise of the civil and political attributes of citizenship. These battles had not been won easily or without resistance. Each progressive thrust has been followed by reactionary counter-thrusts and setbacks.
>
> The struggle for *civil* liberty was opposed, after the French Revolution, by those fearful that it could only lead to tyranny; the fight for *political* participation for fear that it would bring about enslavement to the masses. We are now witnessing one of these counter-attacks on the *economic* liberties of the welfare state, and on some fronts partial retreat.[3]

2   Albert O. Hirschman, *The Rhetoric of Reaction: Perversity, futility, jeopardy*, Cambridge MA, Harvard University Press, 1991.

3   Paul Patrick Streeten, *Thinking About Development*, the 1991 Raffaele Mattioli Lectures, Cambridge, Cambridge University Press, 1995, pp. 275–6.

My own view of history, and of the sources of progress, is different. The notion of trying to ensure 'minimum standards' of material welfare is not in question. What is debatable is the presumption that in an economy of today this depends on collective action, that progress which falls under the heading of 'human development in the *social* and *economic* sphere' has to come largely through deliverance from above.

At best, this is no more than a partial view. It leaves out of account, or at any rate undervalues, what have been, and still remain, the twin leading influences on the material aspect of human development. These are, first, the growth of output in relation to human effort, and second, advances in knowledge and the development of new and improved products, services, methods, techniques and capabilities: the two go together, and both are linked to, and depend on, economic freedom. What Streeten calls the 'social' dimension of human development is in fact largely if not entirely economic. Perhaps the main economic lesson of the past half-century is that in any country where peace and order are maintained, property rights are established and respected, and markets are allowed to be the main influence on the direction of economic activity, the material welfare of virtually everyone can be expected to increase at rates which by earlier historical standards are strikingly high. It seems odd, therefore, to single out the twentieth century as the one in which the most notable advance was to visualise social and economic progress in terms of collective provision.

My main point here was made some time ago by Martin Wolf in the *Financial Times* (8 December 1999). Apropos of the current slogan that capitalism and the market economy need to be given a 'human face', he wrote: '… a dynamic international economy already has a human face. Its humanity derives from the economic opportunities it offers to ordinary people'.

According to the Hirschman–Streeten view, the market-oriented reforms of recent decades are to be seen as 'reactionary', a turning back of the clock of progress. I think there is truth in the idea of a reaction, but not in the assumption that this has meant regress. In the former communist countries, and in China also, there has been a reaction against the twin beliefs that

- state-directed planning is superior to an economic system that rests on private property
- progress consists in the gradual elimination of market-based economic activity.

There are good reasons for viewing this reaction as one of the most hopeful events of the twentieth century. In the rest of the world, there has likewise been a reaction against (for example) monopoly state enterprises, exchange controls, licensing systems, and controls over prices and interest rates. The resulting shifts in policy have not been inspired by a wish to recreate a supposedly golden past. Rather, they have arisen from two main sources: first, some harsh lessons of experience; and second, technical and economic changes which have opened up new possibilities. As time goes on, there may likewise be a reaction against the long-accepted view that the state should be a monopoly supplier of free or heavily subsidised health and education services. If so, this is likely to result from a growing realisation that better results could be achieved, in these areas as elsewhere, by widening the domain of markets, competition and free choice. To react against a model that has outlived its usefulness is not a sign of unenlightened resistance to change.

What is to be done?

On reading the work of some of my colleagues in the profession who are worried about the reforms of recent decades, I am left in doubt as to where they stand. As to the past, do they (for example) want to restore inefficient old-style state monopolies like British Telecom, re-establish exchange controls, bring back fixed stock-exchange commissions, re-impose the virtual prohibitions on imports of coal and the use of natural gas in power stations, re-regulate long-distance bus services, restore the legal privileges and immunities that British trade unions held in 1979, bring back the National Dock Labour Scheme, re-impose the high marginal rates of direct taxation of twenty years ago, refuse to go ahead with the reductions in import barriers that were agreed in the Uruguay Round, or (in Europe) to break up the Single Market? To add some Australian supplementary questions to the list, does Geoff Harcourt want to denounce the Closer Economic Relations Agreement with New Zealand, to go back to the days under Malcolm Fraser when the effective rate of protection for textiles and clothing was 180 per cent, or to restore the restrictive 'two-airline' regime for domestic air services?

Similar questions relate to the future.

- Do the critics favour a continuance of the present Common Agricultural Policy in Europe, together with its counterparts in the US, Canada and Japan?
- Do they want to see a continued or even increasing resort across the world to anti-dumping actions or export subsidies?
- Do they look forward to progressively more far-reaching minimum international labour standards, with provision for their enforcement?

- Do they hope to see an ever-wider range of even more intrusive regulations on businesses?
- Are they content to think in terms of continuing state monopoly provision in education, health and social services?
- Do they want further inroads to be made on freedom of contract in the market for labour services?

Conclusion

On many of these issues, I suspect – indeed, I hope – that there may in fact be a good deal of common ground between those economists who think of themselves as liberals and those who do not, especially when the latter are admirers of Adam Smith. But the main impetus behind anti-liberalism 2000 does not come from within our profession, even though a good many of its members lend support to the cause. Rather, anti-liberalism 2000 draws its strength from the overlapping influences that I have sketched out above, ancient and modern. Under the former heading are the unceasing and determined efforts of pressure groups; the support that often comes to them from disinterested outsiders; and the continuing hold of pre-economic ideas and assumptions. Today these influences link up with the wide-ranging alliance, from NGOs to CEOs, of those who accept the alarmist consensus, focus on perceived disparities, and wish to see the world more closely regulated in the name of sustainability and social justice.

COMMENTS ON THE WINCOTT LECTURE 2000

G. C. HARCOURT

May I say how delighted I am to have been invited to comment on David Henderson's Wincott Lecture? Our friendship dates back to the early 1960s and although it is obvious (or soon will be) that we do not always agree, this in no way affects my respect and affection for him. Now down to brass tacks.

First, let me indicate where we agree – this may take longer than you think! As he says, we both admire our founder, Adam Smith, and I am sure that David has read *The Theory of Moral Sentiments* as well as *The Wealth of Nations* and recognises how complementary the respective messages of the two volumes are to one another. That Smith was revising *The Theory of Moral Sentiments* in the last years of his life is not, I think, an accident; for implementing its findings of the need to create institutions which allow altruism to flourish was, he believed (so do I and, I think, David too), a necessary condition for institutionalising self-interest in a freely competitive environment in society. (Incidentally, Smith was not a democrat – Demos for him was *at best* third, behind Philosopher Kings (no Queens), second and rank and wealth, first. I am a passionate democrat but I also believe that democratic institutions may be coupled with a number of different ways of organising economic and social life, of which the free market model of parts of the advanced industrialised world is only one possibility.)[1]

Secondly, in the policy recommendations I have made, I have

tried to take on board David's fears of imposition from the top and the dangers associated with civil services and bureaucracies generally, in which Buchanan-type civil servants dominate rather than surrogate Keyneses imbued with 'the presuppositions of Harvey Road' as Roy Harrod put it so memorably. Incidentally, this is one of the reasons why when in the 1970s I was asked to be, first, Governor of the Reserve Bank of Australia and, secondly, Head of the Federal Treasury, I said no to both. The main reason was explicit recognition that the Peter Principle would operate in my case but I also thought (as did Peter Karmel and Eric Russell) that I would not survive in an atmosphere in which there was deep resentment by tough and intelligent insiders against an outsider brought in by a political party (I am no Ed Balls). Nevertheless, I want to say that the concept and provision of an incorrupt civil service are perhaps the most important idea/institution which the Brits have bequeathed to the world. Moreover, it is an institution to which free market principles are not especially suited – to put it mildly – for achieving an optimum performance in fulfilling its roles in society. The scathing attacks on civil servants and their roles in recent years are unfair and, socially, potentially extremely dangerous.

Thirdly, I agree with David that creating an environment in which legitimate initiative and enterprise may flourish is of inestimable value for raising living standards and expanding the life choices of all strands of society. That idea is one with which Smith grappled and which he analysed with insight and flair; it is a lesson which, if it were to be unlearned, could have disastrous consequences for the societies concerned. But although I support the

---

1   See G. C. Harcourt, 'What Adam Smith really said', in *Capitalism, Socialism and Post-Keynesianism. Selected Essays of G. C. Harcourt*, London, Edward Elgar, 1995, pp. 230–8.

basic idea, I have severe doubts about the efficacy of the trickle-down hypothesis and the unblemished virtues of unfettered competition in the product and labour markets. After all, both Hayek and Friedman distinguished labour services from the human beings providing them (as did Marx) and while they recognised that competition must be able to eliminate failure as well as reward success, they also insisted on the provision of landing pads, albeit Spartan ones, for the human beings ejected in the process.

Let me deal next with some of the specific points raised by David. First, my conjecture (which I initially put forward in a letter to the *Financial Times* in the early 1990s) that credit for all, though a private good, may be a systemic public bad. My former colleague at Cambridge, the late John Wells (on whose shoulders descended the mantle of Nicky Kaldor with regard to writing letters to the editors of the principal broadsheets) showed me some statistics about the UK which were not inconsistent with the inferences I had made. But I readily accept that these tendencies may have been more than offset by the effects of other factors present in the recent experiences of the OECD economies as David argued. (If Karl Popper spins uneasily in his grave at this defence, so be it.)

Secondly, when I argued for a middle way, I was suggesting the need for balance. For example, though terrible in so many ways the USSR *et al.* were, nevertheless their old people were on the whole secure, the health of their citizens was looked after and technical education was often good though within constraints imposed by the state which I, and I am sure all of you, would have regarded as far too narrow and self-serving. The rush approach to transition following the advice of many western economists has been disastrous for the most vulnerable members of their societies; with more forethought and less haste, much of this could have been avoided. To make a world safe for spivs surely cannot have been anyone's intention?

David stresses the high priority that he gives to freedom of contract, especially in the labour market. There is almost a Hayekian fervour in his advocacy and much substance in what he has to say. Other things being equal, freedom of choice has always to be encouraged. But included in the *ceteris paribus* pound must be some notion of relative equality, or rather relative powerlessness on both sides of a transaction. I am reminded of Joan Robinson's saying to the effect that she did not need the labour theory of value to explain that chaps who owned the means of production and who had access to finance could push around chaps who did not. So I do not see why, for example, when free or freer trade is being extended this should not be coupled with requirements about minimum standards in labour markets. And when discussing, for example, the implementation of realistic minimum wage levels, the findings of the efficiency wage literature for both developing and developed countries should be borne in mind. If individual productivity is affected by levels of real wages and conditions of work generally, the application of simple supply and demand analysis to the labour market is problematic, to say the least. I am sure that David recognises this proviso, but it is not to be found in his text as such.

I don't think I can be included amongst those David calls the new millennium collectivists, but I do belong to a tradition of political economy which takes in Walras, Pigou and James Meade as well as the classical political economists, and, obviously, Keynes and his pupils – Richard Kahn, Austin and Joan Robinson, and, at one remove, Nicky Kaldor and his *alter ego* Tommy Balogh; and my Australian mentors, especially Eric Russell. To these must be added Michal Kalecki – I regard him as probably the greatest all-round economist of the twentieth century – and the analysis by his mentor Marx of the laws of motion of capitalist society (but not of socialist or communist society!).

Let me remind you that Walras believed that land and durable goods should be nationalised, and he confined the competitive market to the production of consumption goods. Taken together, he argued that this would create a *sustainable* equilibrium of efficiency and equity. James Meade's Lib/Lab package deals of policies are the direct descendants of Walras's insights, to which he added Marshallian/Pigovian carrot and stick incentives to guide individual behaviour in socially desirable ways. (Neither Meade nor I was ever doctrinaire on nationalisation.) Keynes was, of course, a liberal who became more conservative with age. Nevertheless, he did not believe that advanced monetary production economies left to themselves created optimum overall employment levels and he wished to have international institutions to guide both employment and trade and capital flows in a broad manner. He recognised that detailed tinkering was a great danger because it opened the way to bribery and corruption as well as to inefficiencies. Nevertheless, measures directed at overall levels of activity and their broad compositions did not imply an intolerable interference with individual liberty and choice. (This was also Meade's view.) Nor did they to Kalecki with his vision of a democratic socialist society which the Stalinists who ran Poland prevented him from trying to help create. I stand fair square with Keynes on this and in doing so I think I have learnt a lot not only from him but from his true modern heirs, for example, Nicky Kaldor and Joe Stiglitz.[2]

---

2   See my 1997 Colin Clark Memorial Lecture, 'Economic Theory and Economic Policy: Two Views', *Economic Analysis and Policy*, 27, 1997, 113–30.

I have just put together for Palgrave all the papers I have ever written on policy, from the 1950s to the present day. Always I have looked for package deals which allow citizens to reach their full potential and to stop the effects of malfunctioning falling most harshly on those least able to defend themselves. That is why I have reserved my ire for those who in the name of freedom and competition have used the deliberate creation of unemployment as the principal way to tackle inflation. This served simultaneously to push the balance of social, economic and political power back to capital and away from labour (who had acquired it during the years of the long boom) and also made the sack an effective weapon of capitalism again (as Kalecki had predicted in 1943). This does not mean that I agreed with the use and abuse of union power. In the 1970s in my own country (Australia) I was appalled at the irresponsibility of such behaviour and said so publicly in hostile forums. Nevertheless I could never go along with Friedman who would rid us completely of unions but who turns a much kinder eye on large firms, arguing that in a world context they are akin to the small price-takers of the modern competitive model.

In other places I have set out the conditions which have to be satisfied for markets to do their thing optimally.[3] And I have queried whether the long-period competitive equilibrium model is a good guide both to understanding modern economies and for providing the basis for development of appropriate policies. Much of David's analysis does, I think, rest on the assumption that it is a good starting point and he does not seem to me to take enough account of the rival model associated with cumulative causation

---

3   See, for example, the policy chapters in *Capitalism, Socialism and Post-Keynesianism. Selected Essays of G. C. Harcourt*, London, Edward Elgar, 1995.

processes. These have their origin in the classical political economists and in some of Marshall's writings; they were spelt out by Allyn Young and Myrdal and developed by Kaldor, Kalecki, Richard Goodwin and others. I may be doing David an injustice but I do think this is a crucial point because which view is believed to be the more relevant explanation makes a huge difference to attitudes to package deals and individual policies.

David seems to me to be too hard on NGOs; he sees them as often economically ignorant and usually top-down authoritarians. If anything I would have thought them too anarchic but often with the right instincts to try to give the underprivileged and oppressed more power over their own lives and decisions, sometimes a throwback to the cooperative movements of the nineteenth century which were admired by both J. S. Mill and Marshall. I may be biased, of course, because our daughter Wendy works for SID and I have been much influenced by her writings – but I don't think so!

Finally, a word on tariffs: of course I would not wish to raise them or to go back to the extraordinary levels of effective protection which he quotes for parts of Australian industry. But I would go very easy on drastic cuts *in one go*, especially when protected industries are concentrated in particular areas. Structural changes require gradual processes, not short sharp shocks, especially when there is no longer a commitment to full employment and many of our economies are not anywhere near full employment. Perhaps I could add that the orders of magnitude of the income elasticities of demand are often much greater than those of price elasticities, so that a world economy growing in unison may bring far more universal benefits than tariff cuts.

To sum up: it is a privilege to comment on David Henderson's thoughtful and thorough analysis. I applaud his emphasis on matching principles and theories with careful empirical investigations. Keynes used to say: 'When someone persuades me I am wrong, I change my mind. What do you do?' I hope this admirable maxim has run through these comments and will do so through any subsequent discussions. But I fear some of you will say, we would not bet on it. In which case may I remind you of Ricardo's last letter to Malthus (31 August 1823)?

> And now, my dear Malthus, I have done. Like other disputants after much discussion we each retain our own opinions. These discussions however never influence our friendship; I should not like you more than I do if you agreed in opinion with me. (Sraffa with Dobb edn, vol IX, Cambridge University Press, 1952, p. 382)

RESPONSE TO COMMENTS

DAVID HENDERSON

I would like to thank Geoff Harcourt for his characteristically fair-minded and courteous comments on my talk. I look forward to pursuing our exchanges. Here I shall respond only on two issues which he has rightly singled out as the main areas of disagreement between us. One is labour market regulation and freedom of contract. The other is the uses and limits of a market economy.

Labour market regulation and freedom of contract

On labour markets, each of us starts from a general proposition. I said that freedom of contract was a leading principle of economic liberalism. He says that it is not a principle to be insisted on, chiefly though not only because employers typically hold the upper hand when it comes to bargaining.

Are the dice chronically loaded against employees? It seems to me that this depends, in large part, on two interrelated factors.

- First, it depends on how far potential employees have a genuine choice between different employers. I believe that many of the economic reforms of recent years have been a positive factor here. Privatisation, deregulation of industries and occupations, competitive tendering for public services, and the freeing of foreign direct investment flows have brought a widening of choice and opportunity. They have reduced the number of firms with monopoly power, weakened the monopoly power of the state as employer, and expanded possibilities for the creation of new enterprises. On the other side of the account, the continuing trend towards closer regulation of businesses in general, which I referred to in my talk, acts as a deterrent to business initiatives that would create new job opportunities. Liberalisation improves the bargaining position of workers, while regulation tends to weaken it.

- Second, the bargaining situation of workers also depends on how tight the labour market is, and this in turn is related to the unemployment rate. Here there is clear evidence, most notably from the OECD Jobs Study, that what one might call the core unemployment rate is kept higher than it need be by labour market regulations, such as laws relating to minimum wages and unfair dismissals.

Geoff argues in general terms for the laying down of compulsory minimum labour standards. I invite him to comment in due course on the examples I quoted from east Germany and South Africa today, as also perhaps on the case of the Australian aboriginal workers whose jobs on cattle stations in the northern tropics were destroyed in the 1960s by the wage regulations then imposed.

Uses and limits of a market economy

Geoff makes the point that the conditions for free markets to work 'optimally' are strict and may well be far from being met in the world as we know it. There are deep analytical waters here, which he has explored more fully than I have. My only comment concerns the direction of change. I believe that the economic reforms of recent years have improved the functioning of markets, and that to carry such reforms forward would bring further improvements. I do not think that this judgement rests on an assumption that the economic system is best described in terms of what Geoff refers to as 'the long-period competitive equilibrium model' – and I note that he himself is inclined to favour tariff reductions, provided that these are gradual rather than sudden.

In this connection, and by way of complementing Geoff's nice concluding quotation from David Ricardo, let me quote another nineteenth-century economist and thinker whom both he and I admire – though he is more of a disciple than I am – and who was certainly not a devotee of any 'equilibrium model'. The excerpt can be seen as pointing the way to a possible next stage in the process of economic reform across the world.

> 'Elementary education by the state' is altogether objectionable. Defining by a general law the financial means of the elementary schools, the qualifications of the teachers, the branches of instruction, etc., and ... supervising the fulfilment of these specifications by state inspectors, is a very different thing from appointing the state as the educator of the people! Government and church should rather be equally excluded from any influence on the school.

These words were written in 1875 by Karl Marx, in his *Critique of the Gotha Programme*.

Besides points of disagreement, I detected in Geoff's comments an implicit criticism which I accept. I said at the beginning of my talk that the treatment was 'admittedly incomplete'. Reading the comments made me realise that it was more incomplete than I had admitted. On a specific point that Geoff raised, I agree that there is more to be said about NGOs than that most of them are anti-liberal, though that is true and important. But there is also a more general point that I would like to touch on in conclusion.

In criticising anti-liberalism from a liberal standpoint, I do not wish to imply that the issues and choices are straightforward, nor that there is a single liberal alternative which is well defined and fully agreed. Economic liberalism comprises a set of ideas and guiding principles. It does not offer a detailed blueprint for all seasons and all countries, and there are different schools of thought within it. Finding a balance between individualism and what I will term 'communitarianism' (since this is more neutral than 'socialism' or 'collectivism') raises many issues which I have not discussed or even referred to today.

Let me end on a note of agreement. All our doctrines and ways of thinking are in a sense provisional: they have to meet the test of experience in a world that is both highly complex and subject to unceasing and often unforeseen change. This was the thought which Geoff Harcourt voiced at the end of his much-appreciated comments; and in this, as on the wisdom of Adam Smith, we have no difficulty in agreeing.

THE WINCOTT MEMORIAL LECTURES

ABOUT THE IEA

The Institute is a research and educational charity (No. CC 235 351). Its mission is to improve understanding of the fundamental institutions of a free society with particular reference to the role of markets in solving economic and social problems.

The IEA achieves its mission by:

- a high quality publishing programme
- conferences, seminars and lectures on a range of subjects
- outreach to school and college students
- brokering media introductions and appearances
- other related activities

Established in 1955 by the late Sir Antony Fisher, the IEA is an educational charity, limited by guarantee. It is independent of any political party or group and is financed by sales of publications, conference fees and voluntary donations.

In addition to its main series of publications the IEA also publishes a quarterly journal, *Economic Affairs*, and has two specialist programmes – Environment and Technology, and Education.

The IEA is aided in its work by a distinguished international Academic Advisory Council and an eminent panel of Honorary Fellows. Together with other academics, they review prospective IEA publications, their comments being passed on anonymously to authors. All IEA papers are therefore subject to the same rigorous independent refereeing process as used by leading academic journals.

IEA publications enjoy widespread classroom use and course adoptions in schools and universities. They are also sold throughout the world and often translated/reprinted.

Since 1974 the IEA has helped to create a world-wide network of 100 similar institutions in over 70 countries. They are all independent but share the IEA's mission.

Views expressed in the IEA's publications are those of the authors, not those of the Institute (which has no corporate view), its Managing Trustees, Academic Advisory Council members or senior staff.

Members of the Institute's Academic Advisory Council, Honorary Fellows, Trustees and Staff are listed on the following page.

The Institute gratefully acknowledges financial support for its publications programme and other work from a generous benefaction by the late Alec and Beryl Warren.

The Institute of Economic Affairs
2 Lord North Street, Westminster, London SW1P 3LB
Tel: 020 7799 8900. Fax: 020 7799 2137
Email: iea@iea.org.uk Internet: iea.org.uk